AWESOME FORCES OF NATURE

TERRIFYING TORNADOES

Revised and updated

Louise and Richard Spilsbury

www.raintreepublishers.co.uk
Visit our website to find out more information about Raintree books.

To order:

Phone 0845 6044371
Fax +44 (0) 1865 312263
Email myorders@capstonepub.co.uk

Customers from outside the UK please telephone +44 1865 312262

©Raintree is an imprint of Capstone Global Library Limited, a company incorporated in England and Wales having its registered office at 7 Pilgrim Street, London, EC4V 6LB - Registered company number: 6695582

"Raintree" is a registered trademark of Pearson Education Limited, under licence to Capstone Global Library Limited

Second edition first published in hardback and paperback in 2010

Edited by Megan Cotugno, Abby Colich, and Andrew Farrow
Designed by Richard Parker
Original illustrations © Capstone Global Library 2004
Illustrated by Geoff Ward
Picture research by Hannah Taylor
Production by Alison Parsons
Originated by Capstone Global Library Ltd
Printed and bound in China by Leo Paper Products Ltd

ISBN 978 0 431178 78 3 (hardback)
14 13 12 11 10
10 9 8 7 6 5 4 3 2 1

ISBN 978 0 431178 85 1 (paperback)
14 13 12 11 10
10 9 8 7 6 5 4 3 2 1

British Library Cataloguing in Publication Data
Spilsbury, Louise.
Terrifying tornadoes. -- 2nd ed. -- (Awesome forces of nature)
1. Tornadoes--Juvenile literature.
I. Title II. Series III. Spilsbury, Richard, 1963-
551.5'53-dc22

Acknowledgements

We would like to thank the following for permission to reproduce photographs: AFP: **21**; Capstone Publishers: **27** (Karon Dubke); FEMA: **28**; Getty Images: **12** (Kyle Gerstner), **20** (Tasos Katopodis), **25** (Kay Chernush); NOAA: **7**, **9**; Photolibrary **15** (OSF/Faidley), **17** (OSF/Faidley); Press Association: **10** (Empics/Rui Vieira), **16** (AP Photo), **19** (AP Photo/Rahman), **23** (AP Photo/Telegraph Herald, Dave Kettering), **26** (AP Photo/Schiappa); Rex Features: **4** (Wayne Hanna), **5** (Houston Post); Science Photo Library: **6** (Eric Nguyen), **14** (Mike Theiss), **24** (Peter Menzel).

Cover photograph of a tornado striking Pampa, Texas, USA in 1995 reproduced with permission of Getty Images (Stone/Alan R Moller).

We would like to thank Dr. Ramesh Srivastava for his invaluable help in the preparation of this book.

Contents

Any words appearing in the text in bold, **like this**, are explained in the glossary.

What is a tornado?

Tornadoes are among the most terrifying forces of nature. A tornado is a fast-moving, spinning column of air that twists down from a thunderstorm cloud. The twisting column of air reaches all the way down to the ground from the cloud in a **funnel**. Many tornadoes look like high, narrow black spinning tops. Other tornadoes look like incredibly long twisted ropes, or even bubbling masses of clouds.

Most of the tornadoes that happen are small. They may last for only a few seconds and do no damage at all. Large tornadoes can be hundreds of metres wide and kilometres high. These tornadoes are the most violent winds on Earth.

This tornado touched down in Canada in 2007. Tornadoes are often called twisters because the winds within them twist and spin.

Spinning winds

Tornadoes can travel at great speeds and they can cause terrible destruction. The spinning winds in the funnel of a tornado act like an enormous vacuum cleaner. They can suck up cars, trains, trees and even houses, and drop them down again from a great height. The winds in tornadoes spin so fast that they can tear buildings apart and flatten whole forests when they pass over.

When a series of six tornadoes hit Houston, Texas, USA, in November 1992, many homes and buildings were severely damaged.

Where did tornadoes get their name?

The word 'tornado' comes from the Latin word *tonare* or the Spanish word *tornar*, which mean 'to twist or turn'. It may also come from the Spanish word *tronada*, which means thunderstorm. These words give a good description of tornadoes – twisting thunderstorms.

What causes tornadoes?

Tornadoes happen when warm, wet winds from one direction meet colder, dryer winds moving in the opposite direction. When these two kinds of winds meet, the warm air rises over the cold air and starts to spin. This is how a tornado starts.

The rising, spinning air sucks in warm air from just above the ground. This warm air becomes part of the tornado. Warm air rises and this makes the tornado rise higher in the air. As it rises, it spins faster and faster. This spiralling part is called the **funnel** or **spout**.

TORNADO FACTS

1. The winds spinning in the funnel of a big tornado may blow faster than any other winds on Earth.
2. Two out of every hundred tornadoes have spinning winds of over 330 kilometres per hour.

The white column of twisting air in this picture is the part of a tornado called the funnel.

What is a tornado like?

A tornado may spin for just a few seconds, or it may go on for several hours. It may spin over one spot for a while and then suddenly dart off in one direction. It is very difficult to tell where a tornado is going next. Sometimes they zigzag about, moving quickly from side to side. Sometimes there are several tornadoes that move in a group or follow each other.

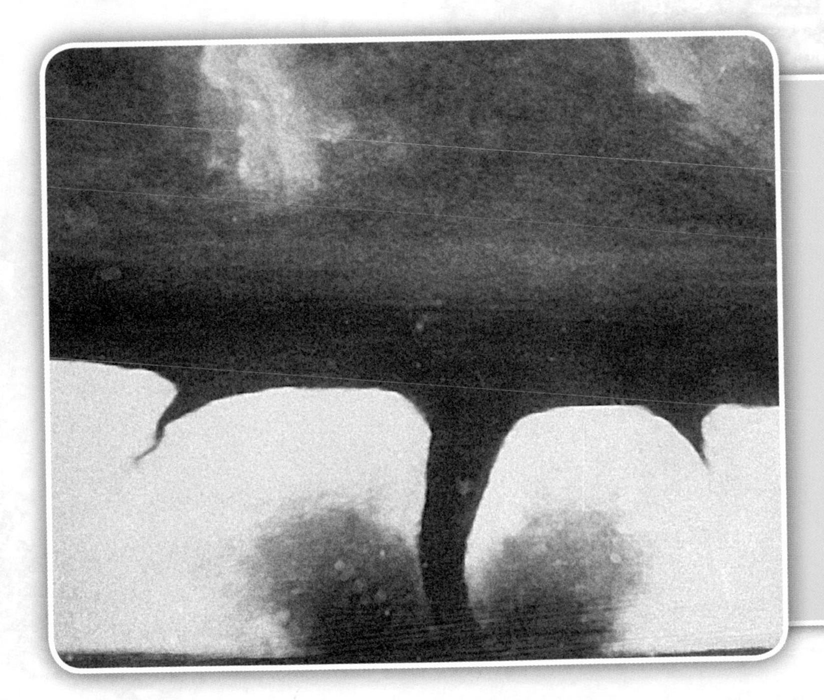

Some tornadoes grow so big that they create other smaller tornadoes. These extra tornadoes can head off on their own. This picture shows the oldest known photo of a group of tornadoes. It was taken in 1884!

What is the difference between a tornado and a hurricane?

Tornadoes and **hurricanes** both have spinning winds, but they are very different forces of nature. A hurricane is a huge storm, but a tornado comes from a storm. Tornadoes can happen in hurricanes. Although they are violent, tornadoes are only very small compared to hurricanes. Tornadoes almost always start far inland, away from the coast. Hurricanes start over warm oceans. Most tornadoes last for less than half an hour, while hurricanes can rage for weeks.

What is a tornado's eye?

The **eye** is the very centre of a tornado. The eye is the point around which the strong tornado winds spiral and twist. It is calm inside the eye. There may be a few clouds and just a gentle breeze. People who have lived through a tornado describe its sound as being like the roaring of many trains or the buzzing of millions of bees. In the eye it may suddenly become quieter.

Some people have seen inside a tornado's eye. They say that when you look up it is like standing at the bottom of a huge pipe. The sides look like a stack of huge, ring-shaped clouds. These clouds are so thick that you cannot see through them.

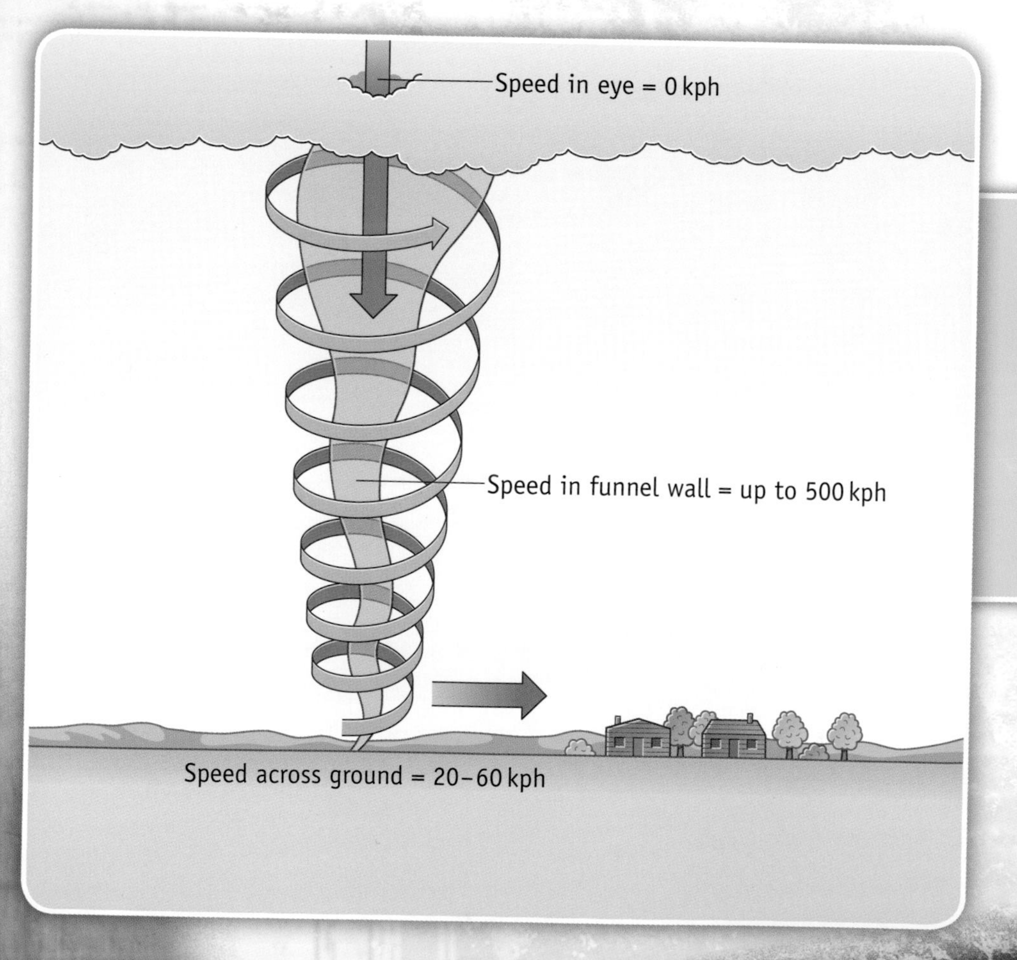

This diagram shows the speeds in different parts of a tornado as it travels across the ground.

What is a waterspout?

Most tornadoes happen far inland, away from water. A **waterspout** is an unusual tornado that forms over an area of water, such as a river, lake, or ocean. This kind of tornado sucks up water as well as warm air.

Waterspouts can be one metre to tens of metres wide. They can be as little as 10 metres high, but the largest waterspout ever seen was over 1500 metres high! Waterspouts usually only last for about 15 minutes. They don't cause as much destruction as tornadoes, but they can seriously damage ships that meet them at sea.

It's raining fish and toads!

Like tornadoes on land, waterspouts pick up objects and drop them down again. Waterspouts have caused showers of toads in France, dropped tadpoles in New York, and once dropped fish from the skies over Rhode Island in the USA!

This is a waterspout off Florida Keys, USA. Most waterspouts look something like this – their thin column-shaped **funnels** sucking water up in the air.

Where and when do tornadoes happen?

Tornadoes can happen anywhere in the world, if the right combination of warm, damp winds meet colder, dryer winds. More tornadoes happen in the USA than anywhere else in the world. Tornadoes also happen in Australia, parts of Europe, such as Italy and the UK, and in Bangladesh and India.

Tornadoes in England!

On average, about 30 tornadoes are reported in the UK each year. Most happen around East Anglia, southern England and the Midlands. On 21 November 1981, a total of 105 tornadoes were reported. This is the highest number of tornadoes to hit any country in Europe in a single day. They happened in the area between Gwynedd, Essex, and Humberside and thirteen were reported in Norfolk alone. Fortunately, none of the tornadoes were big or fast enough to do too much damage.

This photograph shows an aerial view of the damage caused by a tornado in Birmingham, England in 2005.

This map of the world shows where the world's worst tornadoes happen.

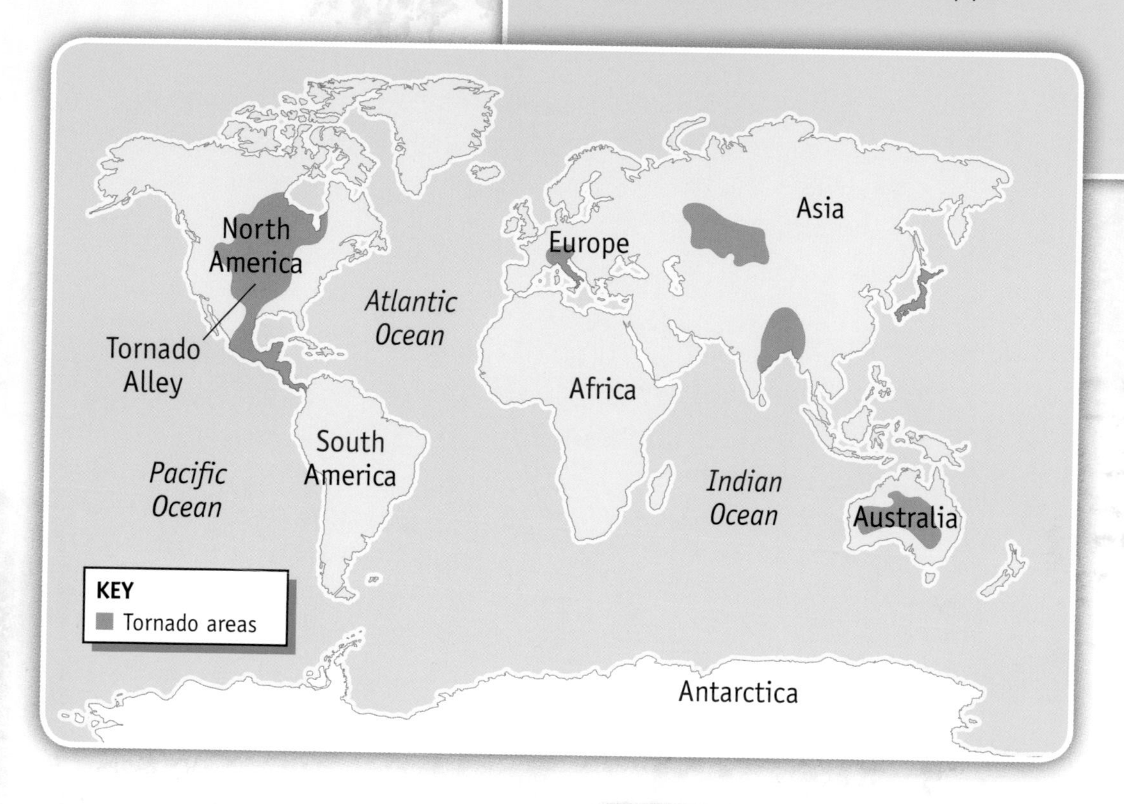

The reason that most tornadoes happen in parts of the USA is the Rocky Mountains! Cool, dry air heading down from Canada is sent eastwards when it hits the huge wall formed by the Rocky Mountains. This cool air then blows over the flat open stretch of land known as the **Great Plains**. Here it crashes into patches of warm, damp air travelling up from the Gulf of Mexico. Tornadoes are so common in this area that it has become known as **Tornado Alley**.

TORNADO FACTS

1. The USA has about 100,000 thunderstorms a year, which cause between 800 and 1000 tornadoes a year.
2. In the USA more than 80 people are killed by tornadoes every year.
3. The Great Plains area in the USA has seven out of ten of all the tornadoes that happen on Earth!

When do tornadoes happen?

In the right wind and weather conditions, tornadoes can appear at any time of the day or night. Most tornadoes, however, start in the afternoon or early evening. This is the time of day when the Sun has warmed up the ground and the air above it. This produces the hot air that is needed to create a tornado.

Tornadoes can also happen at any time of the year, although in many areas they are more common at some times of the year than others. These times are known as **tornado seasons**. In **Tornado Alley** and much of the southern USA, the tornado season happens in spring and summer. Further north, tornadoes tend to come later in the year.

This tornado rips through Conlen, Texas, USA, part of Tornado Alley. It was one of 28 record-breaking tornadoes in the area on 15 May 2003.

Tri-state Twisters, USA, 1925

The Tri-state Twisters were a terrible series of tornadoes that hit the USA on 18 March 1925. The tornadoes came in so close to the ground that people could not see them coming. They looked like big rolling clouds. The twisters raged through three states – Missouri, Indiana, and Illinois – at over 100 kilometres per hour, following a ridge where many mining towns were built.

The Tri-state Twisters were very wide and brought terrible winds and heavy downpours of rain. They wrecked trees, farmland, and buildings. They killed 695 people and injured over 2000. One town, Gorham, in Illinois, was totally destroyed and more than half of the population were killed or injured.

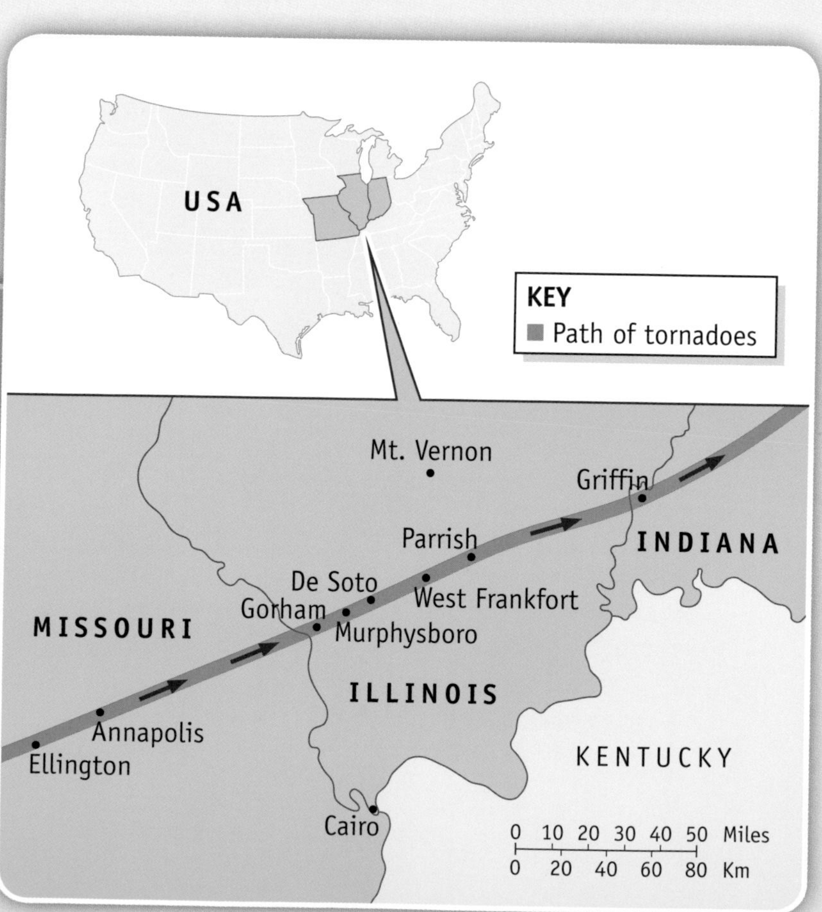

This map shows you the path of destruction followed by the Tri-state Twisters. This set of tornadoes was one of the worst in America's history. They lasted for three-and-a-half hours and finally broke up north-east of Princeton in Indiana.

What happens in a tornado?

People cannot always see the twisting tail of a tornado to tell them danger is on the way. Low storm clouds often hide approaching tornado storms. The first signs that a tornado is coming may be that the sky turns a dark green colour or big **hailstones** fall from the clouds. If you can hear a sound like a rushing waterfall or a roaring jet engine then the tornado is getting very close.

This van was swept away and crushed against several trees during a series of tornadoes that hit Greensburg, Kansas, USA, on 4 May 2007.

TORNADO FACTS

1. A tornado moves like a spinning top. The winds in the **funnel** spin round and round at the same time as the tornado travels across a stretch of land.
2. The winds in the funnel of a tornado can spin at speeds of up to 500 kilometres per hour.
3. A tornado can rush across the ground at up to 110 kilometres per hour, as fast as a moving car.

How do tornado winds cause damage?

Tornado winds break things up and toss them around. Many of the people killed in tornadoes die when objects that are thrown through the air hit them. These winds can blow over walls, **mobile homes**, cars, and trains and they can snap overhead cables and **power lines**, which can be very dangerous. Broken power lines can **electrocute** people or sparks from them may start fires.

The winds in the **funnel** of a tornado have incredibly powerful **suction**. Tornadoes can suck up anything, including millions of tonnes of dust, soil, sand, or roof tiles. They drop them elsewhere when the tornado weakens. When soil and gravel are blown about by tornadoes they cause damage when people breathe them in or get them in their eyes. They can blow against things with such force that they act like sandpaper. They also clog up and **pollute** reservoirs and rivers.

Tornado winds move objects so fast that when they crash into something or someone they can cause serious harm. Even small objects, like this fork that has been **embedded** into a tree, can do a lot of damage.

Tornado strength

The strength of a tornado is judged by its wind speeds. Wind speeds are worked out from the amount of damage that they cause. It is too difficult and dangerous to measure them as they happen. The winds are often so strong that they destroy measuring equipment!

F-0 to F-1 tornadoes cause light to moderate damage to trees and buildings. They break off branches and knock down chimneys. They may also blow **mobile homes** over.

F-2 to F-3 tornadoes cause serious damage. They can tear the roofs off houses, lift and toss cars and overturn trains.

F-4 and F-5 tornadoes are the most violent winds on Earth. They can rip bark off trees, lift and carry whole buildings and throw cars over 100 metres! F-5 tornadoes usually occur only every other year in the USA.

The 'F' used to indicate tornado strengths stands for 'Fujita'. This is because the scale is named after the **scientist** who created it, Dr Tetsuya Fujita. Dr Fujita is pictured here, studying a mini-tornado created in his laboratory.

What is a tornado storm like?

The storms that produce tornadoes bring heavy showers of rain, thunder, and lightning with them. Some have even dropped **hailstones** as big as tennis balls from the sky! Big hailstones like this can cause a lot of damage when they come crashing down to Earth.

When do tornadoes die?

Tornadoes usually break up when they go over colder ground or when the storm clouds above them break up. Most tornadoes only last about 20 minutes and travel less than 25 kilometres. However, some huge tornadoes have travelled 160 kilometres before dying.

Flying cows!

People have told stories of many strange things happening during tornadoes. Hens have had feathers plucked from their backs. Cows have been lifted up, mooing, and dropped down safely far away from their own field. One tornado lifted a pram high in the air and dropped it down again without waking the baby sleeping inside!

Imagine seeing huge hailstones like these falling from the sky towards you! These hailstones fell in Texas, USA.

CASE STUDY

Bangladesh, 1996

At lunchtime on 13 May 1996 in the Tangail district, north-western Bangladesh, the wind suddenly calmed and it got unbearably hot. Then **hailstones** the size of tennis balls fell from the sky as huge thunderstorms built up. These thunderstorms produced a series of terrible and destructive tornadoes. The tornadoes ripped bark from trees, uprooted large trees and caused many buildings to collapse.

Many people in Bangladesh are quite poor and their houses are not very strong. Many houses were built on hillsides out of reach of the floods that often happen during the **monsoon**, the country's wettest season. These houses were hit by the strongest winds.

> “*'The whole village has been reduced to a vast grave.'*
>
> A police officer in Bashail, one of the villages affected”

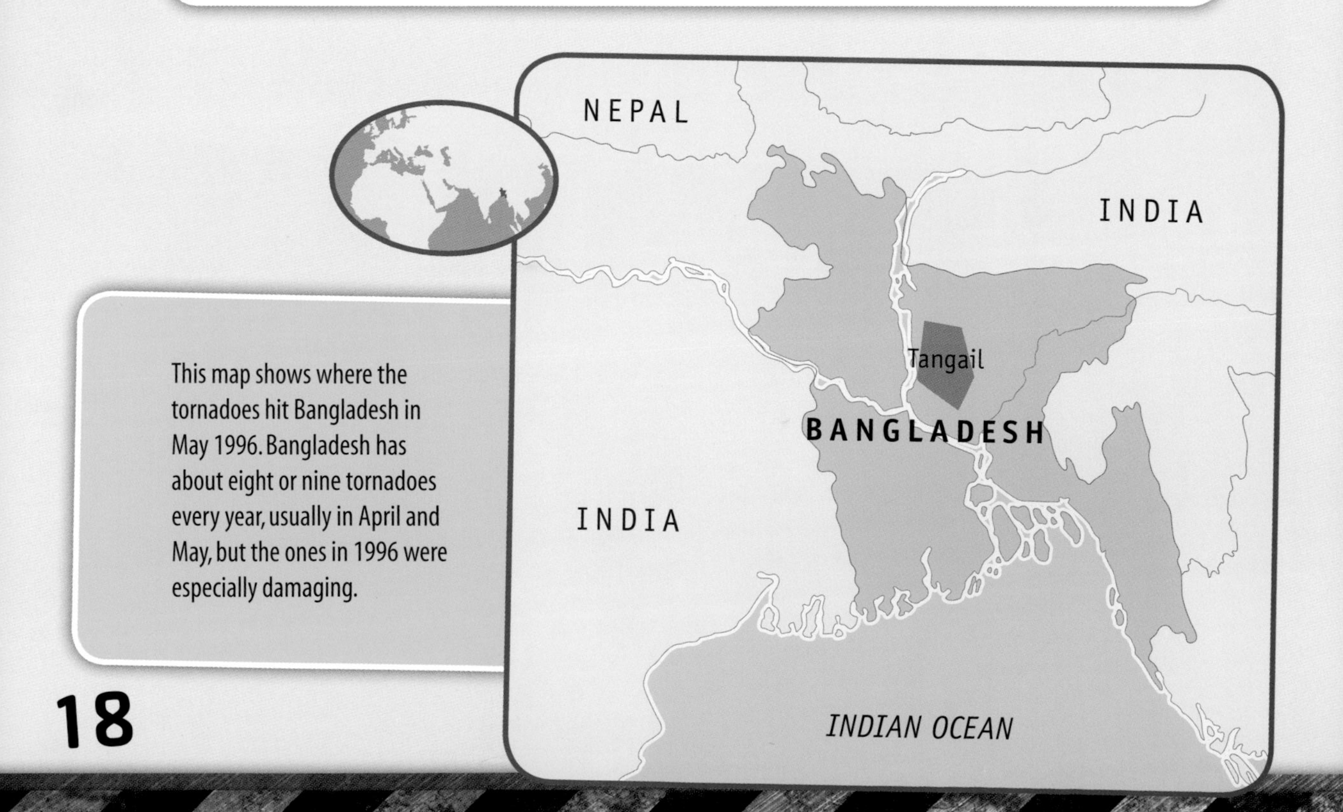

This map shows where the tornadoes hit Bangladesh in May 1996. Bangladesh has about eight or nine tornadoes every year, usually in April and May, but the ones in 1996 were especially damaging.

More than 80 villages and 10,000 homes were destroyed by the 1996 tornadoes in Bangladesh. More than 1000 people were killed and 30,000 people were injured.

Many people had built houses from thin sheets of metal. The tornado broke these up and threw the pieces about. The sharp metal pieces whirled in the air and injured many people. The bad weather and poor roads made it very difficult for rescuers to get to many of the villages. In some villages there were no trucks or buses. People had to carry injured friends and neighbours on their backs or in carts. Because of this, it was a long time before many injured people reached hospitals that could help them. By then their injuries had become infected and many died.

The tornadoes lasted about 2 hours and travelled over 25 kilometres. They left a path of destruction nearly 1.5 kilometres wide.

Who helps after a tornado?

Imagine the scene after a tornado. Houses have collapsed and there is rubbish and **debris** strewn everywhere. Trees have been blown like matchsticks onto roads and buildings. The first people to arrive on a scene like this are rescue workers. They rescue people from cars, **mobile homes**, and crushed houses.

Ambulances and medical workers arrive fast too. They give **first aid** to people who are injured and take those with more serious injuries straight to hospital. Some people will have dust in their eyes or throats which could make them ill. Flying debris may have injured others. Workers from **aid organizations** such as the Red Cross soon arrive. They provide people with the basics – food, clothing, and **shelter**. They also provide food and drink to rescue workers.

Rescue workers may use their hands, spades, chainsaws, or bulldozers to clear bits of wreckage and reach people who are trapped beneath it.

Finding loved ones

Aid organizations such as the Red Cross help people from other places find out if relatives in the tornado-hit area are safe and well. They also help families who were apart when the tornado hit to find each other again.

Clearing up

One of the biggest jobs after a tornado is clearing up the mess. Broken toys, furniture, clothing, fence posts, glass, and crockery are strewn everywhere. Homeowners, **volunteers**, and the Army or **National Guard** may all help. It can take weeks or months just to clear up the debris. When the rubble has been cleared, workers can mend or rebuild homes.

When a tornado hits a **developing country**, people may not have enough money to rebuild their homes or businesses. As well as providing **aid** in the form of food and shelter, aid organizations may also supply tools or other equipment so that people can work and earn money again.

Oklahoma City, USA, 1999

In 1999, several tornados ripped through the US states of Oklahoma and Kansas on Monday afternoon and Tuesday morning of 3–4 May. There were over 70 tornadoes in total. They raged across the land for over 4 hours. At least one of the tornadoes measured 1.5 kilometres across. Winds in some of the tornadoes blew faster than 300 kilometres per hour!

Cars and trucks were thrown around, trees and **power lines** were snapped, and buildings were reduced to rubble. In Oklahoma City, an area called Moore was almost completely flattened. In total, thousands of houses were destroyed and 46 people were killed.

> *'It looks like a bomb hit here. Houses are just levelled [flattened]. It looks like a battlefield.'*
>
> John Ireland, a resident of Moore

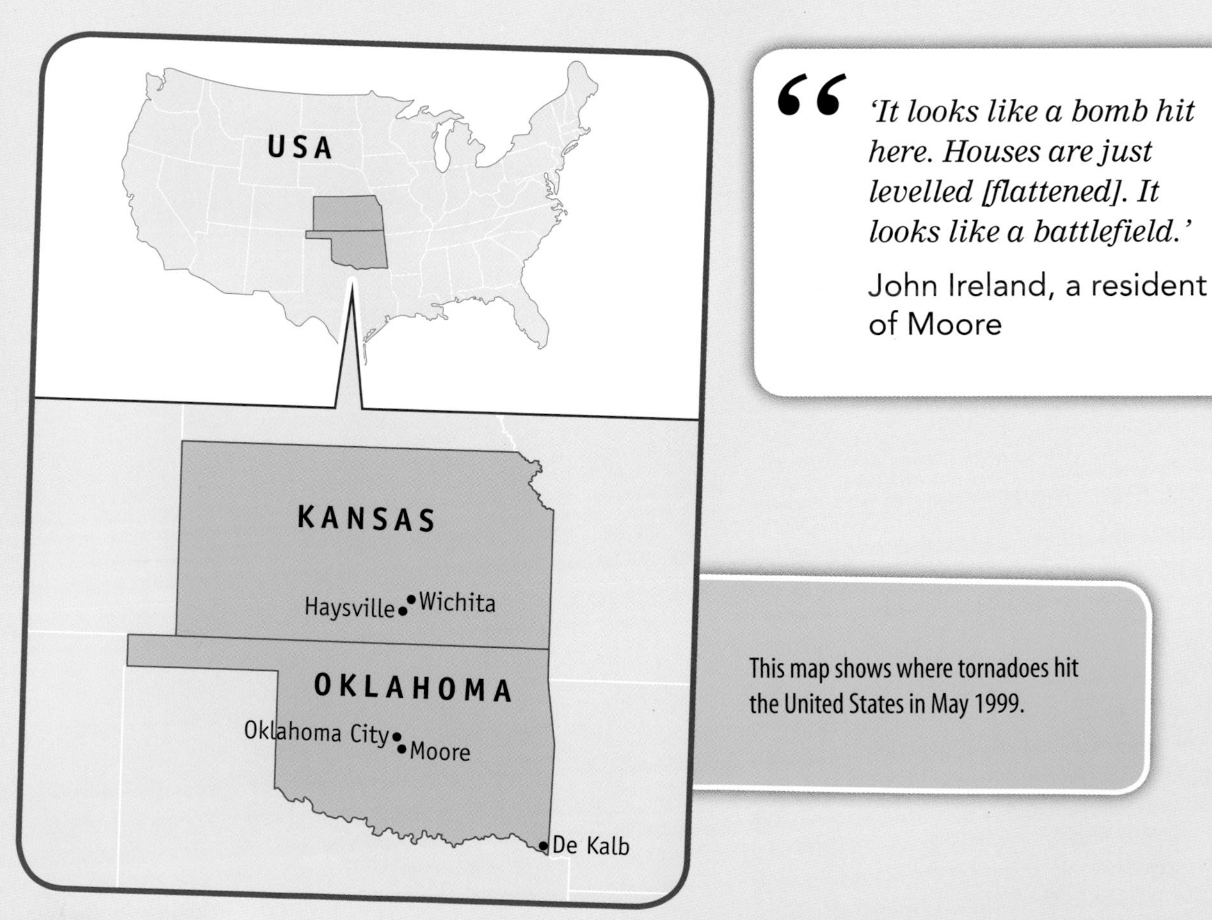

This map shows where tornadoes hit the United States in May 1999.

Who helped in Oklahoma City?

Early TV and radio warnings meant that fewer people died in the disaster than would have been expected. However, many people still needed help. Rescue workers began searching the rubble for survivors straight away. They used dogs to sniff out where people were trapped. Then they used heavy machinery to lift away **debris**. The American Red Cross set up **shelters** for people who had fled their homes or been rescued to spend the night in.

In the weeks after the tragedy, the government provided extra money to create temporary jobs for people whose factories or businesses had been destroyed. They also loaned money to many families so that they could afford to rebuild their homes.

This couple sits outside of what's left of their home after a tornado. They have been given an emergency services kit by the Red Cross.

Can tornadoes be predicted?

It is very hard to tell when a tornado will happen. Often, giant storms that seem likely to create a tornado do not, and small storms that do not usually produce a tornado do! However, **scientists** are working on ways of spotting tornadoes early so that they can warn people to get out of the way.

Weather reports

Weather **forecasters** can tell where storms are gathering and this helps to predict where tornadoes may start. They study pictures taken by **satellites** far above the Earth. These show where swirling clouds and thunderstorms are growing. They also get reports about storms from weather stations that operate in countries all over the world. In some countries there are groups of **volunteers** who watch out for tornadoes and phone weather stations as soon as they see signs of one.

Scientists use weather balloons like this to work out the direction and speed of the wind, high up in the air. This is one of the pieces of the puzzle they put together to work out when a tornado might happen.

Using advanced technology

Scientists use new technology as well as observing the weather to spot tornadoes early. **Doppler radar** is a special piece of equipment that can tell when there are strong spinning winds in a storm. These are the kinds of strong winds that might become a tornado. Scientists also use equipment that can **detect** lightning flashes between clouds even during daylight. They have worked out that faster flashing means a storm is getting worse.

This Doppler radar in Virginia, USA, can help us to detect tornadoes.

Who are storm chasers?

Storm chasers are scientists who find and follow storms. They travel in vehicles with special equipment inside, such as video cameras, Doppler radar and computers. They use this equipment to study how tornadoes behave. The information they collect is very useful for working out what to expect from future tornadoes.

Can people prepare for tornadoes?

Only a small number of tornadoes actually hit people's homes every year, so it is very unlikely that even people in **Tornado Alley** will be affected. However, people who live in areas where tornadoes do happen can take steps to protect themselves.

Can buildings be made stronger?

People can make their buildings stronger and better able to resist tornadoes. They can bolt buildings to firm **foundations** and seal the gaps under roof tiles so winds cannot get underneath them. Many people build special **storm cellars**. These are either basements that are strengthened with concrete and strong doors, or separate rooms under the ground in the garden. People can hide in these during a tornado to be safe.

This is a storm cellar. If people do not have a cellar like this, they should **shelter** in a room on the lowest floor of the house. They should keep away from windows and hide under something sturdy to protect themselves from flying **debris**.

Tornado plans

People should not worry about tornadoes, but they should know what to do if one happens. In the USA, if a 'tornado watch' is announced it means that there is a possibility of a tornado and people should be ready to move to a safe shelter or **evacuate**. A 'tornado warning' means that a tornado has been spotted and people should calmly go to their shelter immediately. Everyone in the family should learn exactly where to go and what to do.

Keep a disaster supply kit in case of an emergency. It should include items such as a radio, bottled water, canned food, batteries, and a torch.

Disaster supplies kit

People in tornado zones are also advised to prepare a disaster supplies kit. This should contain:

- a **first-aid** kit
- a battery-powered radio (as electricity supplies may be cut off)
- a torch (and extra batteries)
- bottled water
- cans and packets of food (and a can opener!)

Can tornadoes be prevented?

Tornadoes are natural disasters that cannot be stopped. The only things people can do to reduce the damage tornadoes cause are to predict them earlier and be better prepared.

At the moment, only about half of all tornadoes can be spotted in time to warn people about them. In the future, **scientists** hope to set up systems across the world that can more accurately predict tornadoes. They are also working on ways to stop tornadoes forming. For example, people have tried firing **dry ice** into growing storms. The idea is to make the storm drop more rain, which makes it weaker. In this way scientists might be able to stop a storm producing any full-blown tornadoes.

In order to reduce the amount of damage tornadoes can do, people need to understand what tornadoes are. This **volunteer** for the US organization **FEMA** is advising a local resident on what to do in the event of a tornado.

Terrifying tornadoes of the past

Comoro Island, 1951
The Comoros Islands off eastern Africa were hit by a strong tornado. About 500 people were killed and the city of Anjouan was flattened.

India and Bangladesh, 1963
A tornado travelling at 80 kilometres per hour touched down in India and passed through southern Bangladesh. In India, 139 people were killed and even more died in Bangladesh. People were picked up and thrown 300 to 600 metres.

Midwestern USA, 1965
On 11 April 1965, about 48 tornadoes crashed through the US states of Iowa, Wisconsin, Illinois, Michigan, Indiana, and Ohio within a period of 12 hours. These tornadoes killed 256 people and caused more than $200 million of damage.

Dhaka, Bangladesh, 1969
Many people live in the city of Dhaka. When a tornado hit the city on 14 April 1969 it killed several people and injured thousands more.

Midwestern USA, 1974
On 3 and 4 April 1974, 148 tornadoes raged for over 16 hours across the centre of the USA through thirteen states, including Ohio and Kansas. Over 330 people were killed and around 5500 people were injured.

Wichita Falls, Texas, USA, 1979
On 10 April 1979, three tornadoes killed 42 people and injured about 1700 more as they travelled across the US states of Texas and Oklahoma. Shopping **malls** and several hundred buildings were destroyed.

Midwestern USA, 1990
Around 50 tornadoes hit the midwestern USA within 4 hours. They killed 65 people and damaged 24 cities, within 7 states, from Wisconsin to Kansas.

Central USA, 2007
Over 100 tornadoes were reported in Kansas and surrounding states on May 4 and 5. After the town of Greensburg, Kansas, was completely flattened, its residents decided to rebuild as an environmentally conscious community.

Glossary

aid help given as money, medicine, food, or other essential items

aid fund collection of money donated by ordinary people and used to provide aid

aid organizations groups of people who work together to raise money and to provide help for people in need

debris loose bits of solid material, such as stones and rocks

detect spot or find

developing country poorer country of the world that is gradually trying to develop better conditions for its people

Doppler radar special machine that uses invisible rays to detect where things are

dry ice frozen carbon dioxide

electrocute kill by electric shock

embedded deeply and solidly lodged into another object

evacuate move people from a dangerous place to somewhere they will be safe

eye calm centre of a tornado (or hurricane)

FEMA stands for 'Federal Emergency Management Agency'. FEMA is an American government agency that is in charge of helping people before and after a disaster.

first aid first medical help given to injured people

forecaster person who predicts the weather

foundation solid base upon which a building is built

funnel spiralling central part of a tornado

Great Plains middle section of the United States

hailstone ball of ice that falls from a cloud during a thunderstorm

hurricane larger tornado-like storm that forms over the ocean

malls shopping centres

mobile home home that can be moved

monsoon wet season in parts of Asia and elsewhere

National Guard volunteer soldiers recruited and trained by each US state

pollute when part of the natural environment is poisoned or harmed by human activity

power line cable that carries electricity

satellite object that goes around the Earth in space. Satellites do jobs such as sending out TV signals or taking photographs.

scientist person who studies aspects of the world around us

shelter somewhere warm and safe to stay

spout cone-shaped tube or pipe. A tornado can also be called a spout.

storm cellar underground room where people can shelter during a tornado

suction sucking power

Tornado Alley southern part of the middle of the US where tornadoes occur frequently

tornado season time of the year when tornadoes happen most often

volunteers people who work without being paid for what they do

waterspout tornado that forms over an area of water

Find out more

Books

Disasters Up Close: Tornadoes, Michael and Mary Woods (Lerner, 2008)
Graphic Natural Disasters: Tornadoes and Superstorms, Gary Jeffrey (Franklin Watts, 2010)
Storm Warning - Tornadoes, Carol Baldwin (Raintree Publishers, 2005)
What on Earth: Tornadoes, David and Helen Orme (Book House, 2006)
Wild Weather: Tornado, Catherine Chambers (Heinemann Library, 2008)

Websites

www.fema.gov/kids/tornado.htm – this website contains facts about tornado dangers, what to do and how to prepare.

www.nationalgeographic.com/eye/tornadoes/tornadoes.html – here you can see video reports from people who have lived through tornadoes.

Index